UNITED STATES ARMY

TRAINING CENTER
FORT DIX, NEW JERSEY

HISTORY OF FORT DIX

Fort Dix is named for Major General John Adams Dix, a 19th Century patriot who served as a United States Senator, Governor of New York, Ambassador to France and Secretary of the Treasury.

"Camp" Dix was officially established July 18, 1917 and designated a cantonment area and training post for troops who would fight in Europe during World War I. It rapidly grew into one of the nation's largest military reservations and trained three divisions and numerous other units during the war.

The camp became a demobilization center following the armistice. From 1922 to 1926, it was a training ground for active Army, Army Reserve and National Guard units and then remained in a caretaker status until 1933. From 1933 to 1939, the post served as a reception, discharge and replacement center for the Civilian Conservation Corps. In 1930, the camp became a permanent Army installation and its name was changed to Fort Dix. It served as a reception center for men inducted under the Selective Service Act of 1939. Ten divisions and many smaller units either trained or staged here prior to assignment on the global battlefields of World War II.

After World War II, the reception center became the separation center, returning almost 1,200,000 soldiers to civilian life. In 1947, Fort Dix was designated a basic training center and later that year became the home of the 9th Infantry Division. In 1954, the 9th was transferred overseas and the 69th Division reactivated at Fort Dix. In March 1956, the 69th was inactivated and Fort Dix was officially named the United States Army Training Center, Infantry.

During the fifties, Fort Dix experienced a tremendous growth and expansion. The 300 family quarters, known as Sheridanville, was completed in February 1952 and in December that same year, another housing project was completed and named Nelson Courts. Among the most notable developments, was breaking of ground for the new 500-bed Walson Army Hospital in 1957. A year later, an innovation in basic training was created with the building of Proficiency Park. The park's mission is to test the infantry skills of every soldier completing basic training.

In March 1959, the infantryman was symbolized with the construction of "The Ultimate Weapon" of the United States Army, when a 3,000 pound statue of the foot soldier was unveiled at Missile Park. A newly constructed 1,004 seat theater was dedicated to the memory of First Lieutenant Karl H. Timmerman, who was awarded the Distinguished Service Cross for his action at the Remagen Bridge in Germany. Another construction project completed during that year was a 702-unit duplex housing development, Garden Terrace. In March 1960, the 10 ½ million dollar, Walson Army Hospital was completed. In its first year of operation, the hospital admitted 23,000 patients.

The overall renovation of the post continued as the temporary wooden buildings, which characterized old "Camp" Dix, disappeared to make way for barracks of brick and cement. Under the master construction plan, Fort Dix was converted from a wooden cantonment station to a modern Army post, with buildings of permanent construction.

Fort Dix' five training regiments were renamed brigades in August 1965. The 1st Training Regiment became the 1st Advanced Individual Training Brigade, the 2d, 3d and 7th Training Regiments became Bas[…] Combat Training Brigades, and the 5[…] Training Regiment was renamed th[…] 5th Common Specialist Trainin[…] Brigade. As a result of a study b[…] former Secretary of the Army, St[…] phan Ailes, another change to th[…] training organization occurred […] October of the same year. The thre[…] basic combat training brigades we[…] reorganized into two brigades and th[…] 4th brigade was discontinued. Also […] the reorganization, Faculty Group w[…] redesignated Committee Group an[…] became a major command. Later […] 1966, the Common Specialist Brigad[…] was renamed the 5th Combat Su[…] port Training Brigade.

Fort Dix expanded rapidly durin[…] the Vietnam War, as once again th[…] American soldier was called upon t[…] defend freedom. As the United State[…] involvement in Vietnam began t[…] close, Infantry AIT was discontinued […] Fort Dix and the 1st AIT Brigade w[…] deactivated in September 1969.

In 1970, the Main Post Exchang[…] Cafeteria was completed and co[…] struction began on the 3.9 millio[…] dollars Confinement Facility. Th[…] Modern Volunteer Army Progra[…] (VOLAR) was initiated in Novemb[…] 1971. The results at Fort Dix wer[…] readily visible in the form of increase[…] services for the soldier and many ne[…] construction projects being comple[…] ed in 1972. Among these were th[…] Doughboy Inn, Post Laundry Facilit[…] and the Indoor Swimming Pool.

During the seventies, Fort D[…] continued to experience significan[…] improvements and reorganization in i[…] installation and training missions. […] 1972, the overall training base wa[…] reduced from 12 battalions and 6[…] companies to 10 battalions and 5[…] companies. The 5th Combat Suppo[…] Training Brigade's name was change[…] to 5th AIT Brigade (CS) and beg[…]

integrating women into its six MOS courses. In 1973, the 2d BCT Brigade was deactivated and the 3d BCT Brigade assumed responsibility for its command and control headquarters and 11 of its companies. The Oversea Replacement Station was closed on 1 June 1973 and the construction of the Reception Station Building was completed that year. In July of 1973, Fort Dix was placed under the newly formed Training and Doctrine Command (TRADOC). In 1974, all STRAF/REFORGER units, with the exception of Military Police, were attached to the 5th AIT Brigade (CS). Effective 1 July 1975, New York Area Command (NYAC)/Fort Hamilton became a sub-installation of Fort Dix, including all military installations that are consolidated under Fort Hamilton.

Fort Dix demonstrated its capabilities to the civilian community in 1977 by providing needed assistance for both the Buffalo Blizzard and the Johnstown Flood, two of the nation's largest natural disasters, which occurred that year. Personnel who participated in these disaster relief programs were awarded the Humanitarian Service Medal for their outstanding service to the preservation of life and property.

New innovations in training came with the advent of Self Paced One Unit Training (SPOTRAIN) in the 5th AIT Brigade, which was reorganized as the 5th Training Brigade in July 1977. In 1978, the 3d BCT Brigade was reorganized as the 3d Basic Training (BT) Brigade. In October of 1978, Fort Dix implemented its latest and most significant change in training philosophy to date, for the new soldier, by integrating women into its Basic Training Program, beside their male counterpart.

Fort Dix has proven to be truly innovative and sensitive to the times. However, the primary mission of training troops has not changed over the years - only the methods to perform that mission, for the betterment of humanity and the American Soldier.

**JOHN ADAMS DIX
MAJOR GENERAL
U.S. ARMY**

ROBERT H. FORMAN
MAJOR GENERAL
U.S. ARMY

MAJOR GENERAL
ROBERT H. FORMAN
U.S. ARMY
BIOGRAPHY

Major General Robert H. Forman was born in Phoenix, Arizona, graduated from Arizona State University, and is a veteran of more than 29 years of active commissioned service.

Major General Forman is an ROTC distinguished military graduate and was commissioned in the Regular Army on 15 June 1951. After attending the Artillery Basic Course, he served with a Field Artillery Battalion at Fort Lewis, Washington, and then was assigned to Korea where he served with the 17th Field Artillery Battalion for 13 months.

After attending the Artillery Battery Officer Course, he was assigned to the 11th Airborne Division and served as a Battery Commander at Fort Campbell, Kentucky, and Augsburg, Germany, and commanded the airborne artillery battery which accompanied the airborne forces to Lebanon during the summer of 1958.

After graduation from the Artillery Advanced Course, he served as an Assistant Professor of Military Science at Seattle University. He then attended the Command and General Staff College in 1964 and later served as a Province Senior Advisor in Vietnam. He then was assigned to the Department of the Army Staff for two years before taking command of a field artillery battalion in the 82d Airborne Division.

Upon graduation from the Army War College in 1970, he was assigned to the faculty of the Command and General Staff College at Fort Leavenworth. While in this assignment, he served as a chairman on the U. S. Army Leadership Board. Later, he was assigned as the G3 advisor for the ARVN II Corps in Vietnam and then as Chief of the U. S. Element of the Joint Military Commission, Region IV.

He commanded the 214th Field Artillery Group at Fort Sill from July 1973 until February 1975. He then was assigned to the Field Artillery School at Fort Sill, first as Director of Doctrine and then Director of Instruction. From June 1976 to July 1979, he served as Deputy Commanding General at U. S. Army Training Center Engineer and Fort Leonard Wood, Fort Leonard Wood, Missouri. In July 1979, he was assigned as Deputy Commandant, U.S. Army Command and General Staff College, Fort Leavenworth, Kansas. In February 1981, he assumed command of U. S. Army Training Center and Fort Dix, Fort Dix, New Jersey.

Major General Forman's decorations include the Legion of Merit (4 awards), Soldier's Medal, Bronze Star with "V" Device (3 awards), Meritorious Service Medal (3 awards), Air Medal with "V" Device (7 awards), Army Commendation Medal (4 awards), and several Vietnamese decorations. He also holds the Master Parachutist Badge, the Combat Infantryman's Badge, Ranger Tab, General Staff Identification Badge, and several service medals.

General Forman and his wife, Hannah Jean, have two daughters; Mona and Nancy, and one son, Robert.

April 1981

MAJOR GENERAL ROBERT H. FORMAN

DEPARTMENT OF THE ARMY
HEADQUARTERS US ARMY TRAINING CENTER AND FORT DIX
FORT DIX, NEW JERSEY 08640

ATZDCG

CONGRATULATIONS

You are now a soldier and fully qualified to join the ranks of the United States Army.

During training here at Fort Dix, you have met challenge after challenge in the true tradition of the spirit which keeps our nation free.

You have acquired the basic character of a soldier by developing confidence in yourself and becoming competent in all basic skills. This confidence and competence, together with your demonstrated self-discipline, will be of great value to you in the future. Keep building on all that you have attained here at Dix.

The officers and noncommissioned officers of your unit are proud of the effort you have displayed and in your accomplishments over the past few weeks.

Our best wishes for continued success go with you.

God speed.

ROBERT H. FORMAN
Major General, USA
Commanding

J. J. BROPHY
BRIGADIER GENERAL
U.S. ARMY

BRIG GEN J. J. BROPHY
DEPUTY COMMANDER

RECEPTION STATION

This is the gateway to the Army. How do they get everything accomplished here? This may be one of the thoughts that occurs in the soldier as they process through the reception station. It becomes quite clear to them that they do get a great deal accomplished during the brief few days stay.

Aptitude test, physical examination, a classification interview, orientation meetings, a clothing issue and the creation of a permanent file- all are completed within the few days of processing at the Reception Station.

The change from civilian to trainee has to be a swift one, for in the next seven weeks they will receive intensive training in the fundimentals of soldiering that may have to be applied in the defense of our country and their own lives.

Even as the soldiers move to the training companies, they have begun to understand a little of the routine that will become such an important part of their seven weeks in Basic Training.

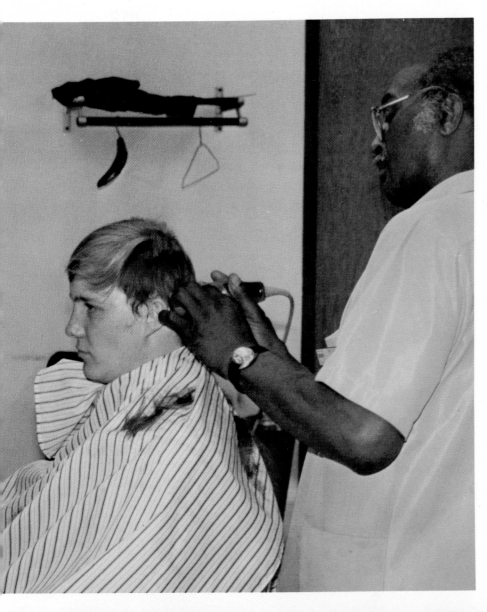

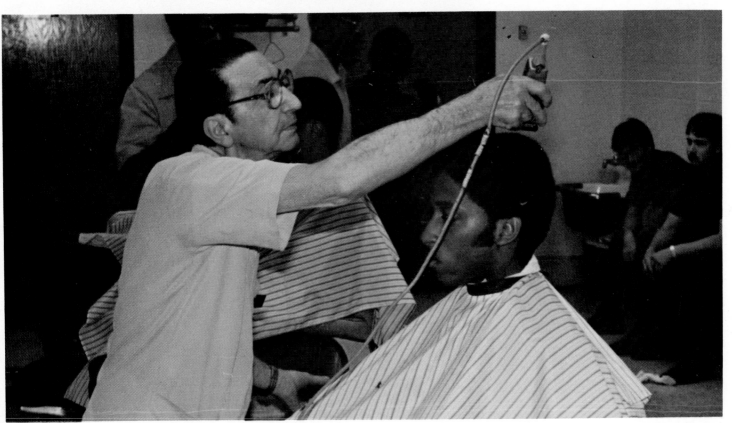

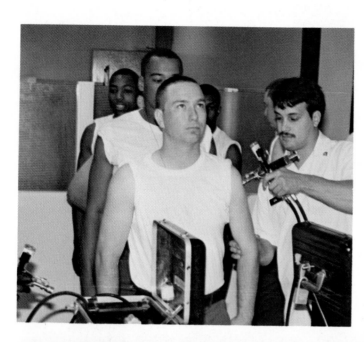

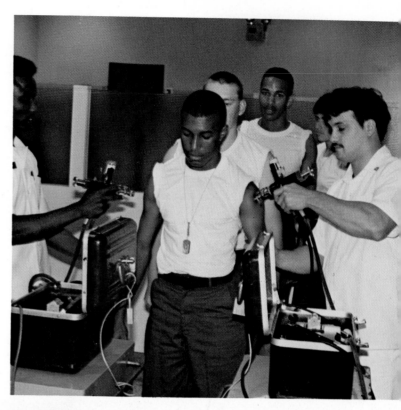

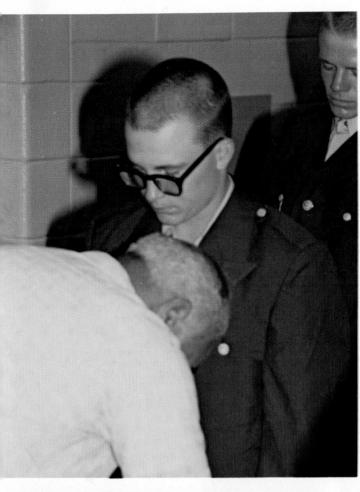

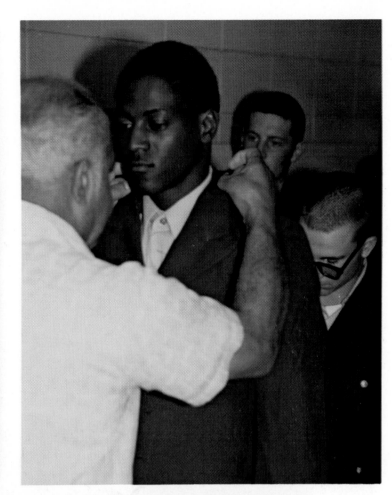

COMPANY AREA

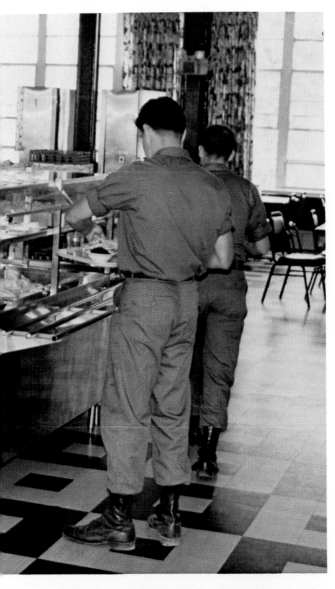

DINING FACILITY

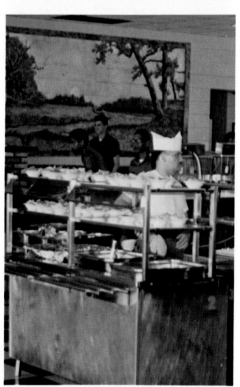

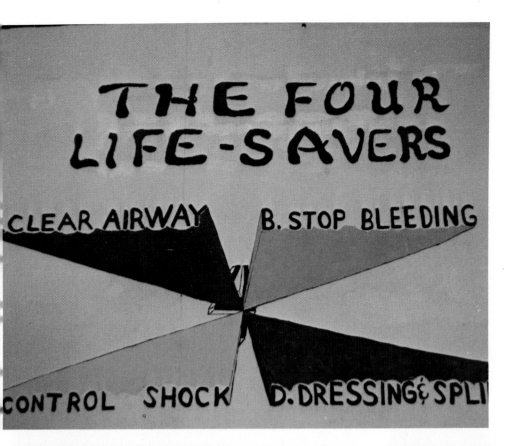

FIRST AID

Soldiers must be versitile and self-reliant. In the clamor of the battle, at a distance from complete medical facilities, a life can depend upon their knowledge of first aid.

Through lectures, demonstrations and practical exercises, the trainees become experts in first aid. They learn to deal with splints, ties and bandages; to give emergency treatment in case of shock, bleeding, fractures, snake or insect bites and drowning. They acquire skills which will prove valuable both in the Army and civilian life.

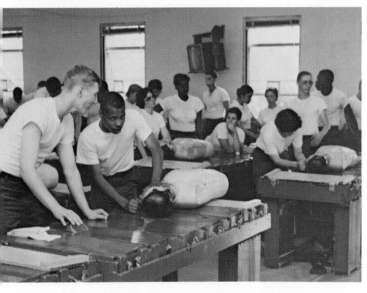

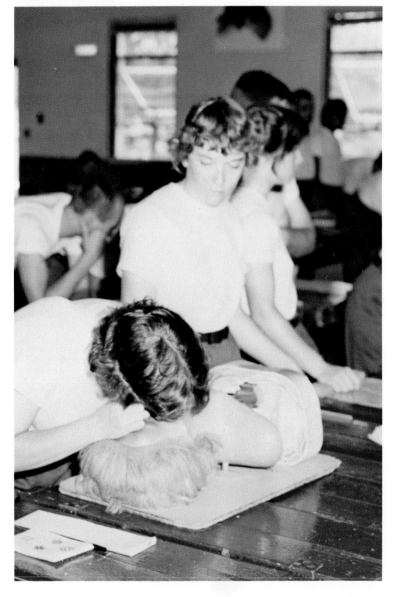

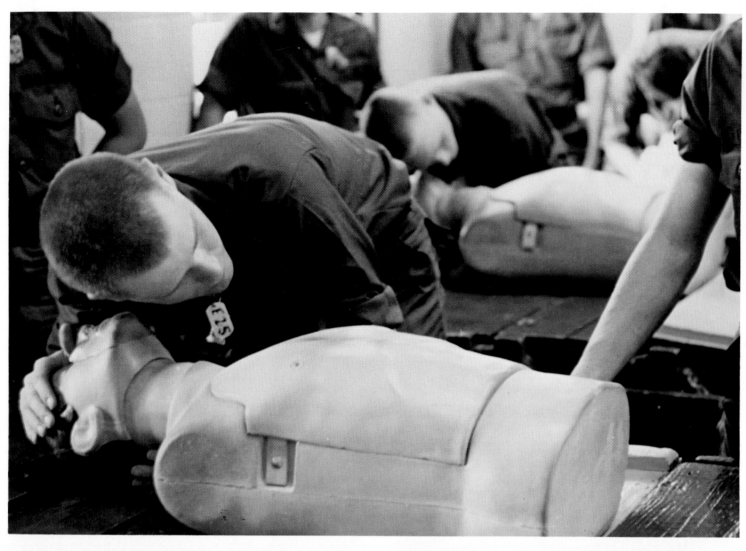

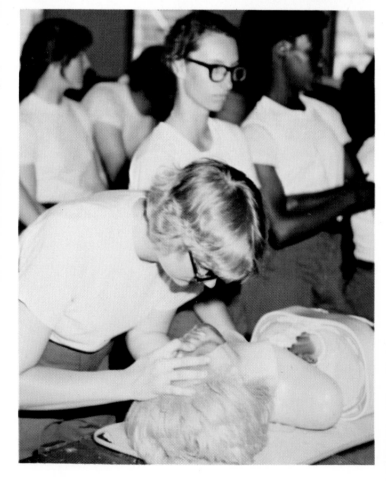

NUCLEAR BIOLOGICAL CHEMICAL

The battlefield of the future - what may it be like? In the face of uncertainty, preparedness is essential. The Army prepares its soldiers with the necessary training in defense against nuclear, biological and chemical agents.

How is the NBC attack recognized? How to protect oneself . . . what first aid measures can be taken? The soldier learns the questions and the answers.

Practical training in the use of the protective mask is an essential part of NBC training. The constant drills pay off, when the word "GAS" is heard.

CONFIDENCE COURSE

OBSTACLE COURSE

FIELD FIRING

The 25-meter range stressed the fundamentals of rifle firing, grounding the soldier in the basic skills of sighting and aiming. In Field Firing, the soldier encounters more complicated conditions.

They learn different firing positions. They encounter the "pop-up" target — the dark silhouette which will become the measure of their firing skill.

Placed at distances from 70 to 300 meters, the targets are centrally controlled to appear and disappear in varied times and sequences.

As the training progresses, it becomes more difficult; the soldier at first knows the target sequence; later dealing with "surprise" targets.

The targets are "killable" - when hit by a bullet, they fall automatically. This system adds interest and realism to the training, and gives the soldier instance evidence of firing accuracy.

FIELD CHOW

HAND GRENADES

Flat on the stomach the soldier feels the ground tremble from the blast of a hand grenade thrown ten seconds earlier. In the block of instruction that precedes this exercise, types, characteristics and capabilities of the grenade are outlined. In addition, rigid safety precautions are enforced. Positions and throw techniques are practiced and lead to throw of a live grenade at a 35 meter target.

M-60
MACHINE GUN

ANTI-TANK

BIVOUAC

People become Soldiers; they no longer walk - they march over grass and sand and clay and gravel; they march to and from training areas, drill fields, classes.

All of the soldier's previous instruction is climaxed by bivouac - encampment exercise in the field. Here they live in a tent community, eat food prepared in the field, practice the skills of the Soldier in the forward battle zone.

They march to the site of the encampment - carrying their weapons and full packs. They test their training by experience, and learn a final lesson: to respect and cherish the most valued pieces of equipment - the feet.

PHYSICAL TRAINING (P.T.)

A soldier must be tough - tough enough to stand a demanding daily routine; tough enough to enter combat with a full measure of strength. Physical fitness, therefore, is an essential part of a Soldier's training.

The physical training program of the U.S. Army is designed to develope strength, endurance, agility, and coordination - and to promote confidence, aggressiveness and team spirit.

What does it take? Miles of running, hundreds of push - ups, dozens of repetitions of the "daily dozen" exercises. The result: strength for a time which demands strength.

DRILL AND CEREMONIES

Sharp commands echo across the drill field and marching feet beat a tattoo across the ground; another order sounds, and dozens of rifles snap in unison. These are the sounds of an institution as old as organized armies; dismounted drill.

The hours spent on the drill field have one aim; to develop in the soldier an instinct for precision, an ingrained habit of obediance to command, a sense of teamwork. They learn squad, platoon, and company drill; the manual of arms, the school of a soldier without arms.

And in the training they acquire habits which are the foundation of all else they will learn in the Army: discipline, alertness, and trigger-quick response.

GRADUATION

THIRD TRAINING BRIGADE

COL F. H. CHANDLER

Brigade Commander

CSM P. D. HOLLIDAY

Brigade Sergeant Major

5TH BATTALION

LTC J. A. C. CASH

Battalion Commander

CSM G. C. CARTER

Command Sergeant Major

COMPANY B

SFC D. Llamas

Senior Drill Sergeant

PSG R. Perez

Platoon Sergeant

SFC C. West

Platoon Sergeant

SSG C. Alston

Platoon Sergeant

SGT B. Fryer

Asst. Platoon Sergeant

SGT H. Williams

Supply Sergeant

CPL J. Pushia

Armorer

No Photos Available

CPT P. Glovas

Company Commander

2LT D. Krause

Training Officer

1SG L. Burgess

First Sergeant

SFC J. Aretz

Platoon Sergeant

SFC W. Plelcher

Platoon Sergeant

SSG L. Ingalls

Platoon Sergeant

SGT N. Pyles

P. Mitchell

Asst. Platoon Sergeant

SGT L. Smith

Asst. Platoon Sergeant

Unidentified
Unidentified
Unidentified
Unidentified
Unidentified

Acececdo, P.
Adams, R.
Alicea, H.
Anderson, D.
Anthony, B.

Anzek, S.
Armstrong, T.
Arnold, T.
Arriola, O.
Avellino, F.

Barnes, A.
Barrus, R.
Becerra, P.
Bechtold, N.
Becker, C.

Bedard, R.
Bellew, P.
Bennett, T.
Bennett, T.
Best, D.

Bivians, D.

Blakley, M.

Blankenship, S.

Boggs, M.

Bouilier, R.

Bourque, D.

Bozung, M.

Breisch, T.

Brigman, S.

Brott, E.

Bryant, D.

Buckley, J.

Burkhalter, C.

Call, G.

Canright, W.

Carson, C.

Carter, R.

Castro, B.

Chalker, M.

Cherie, T.

Christen, Recruit

Clay, J.

Colston, R.

Coluelt, Recruit

Conner, W.

Cooper, P.

Crawford, W.

Dambrose, E.

Davis, J.

Dean, B.

Devaney, W.

Dias, M.

Donnie, B.

Douglas, P.

Earhart, T.

Eblin, P.

Evans, D.

Everett, L.

Ervin, L.

Farrar, D.

Fennell, T.

Fortune, W.

Franklin, Recruit

Frisby, B.

Garviso, J.

Gaudette, T.

Gibbs, R.

Gray, C.

Gray, L.

Green, M.

Greenwood, W.

Hall, D.

Hardin, O.

Hayes, S.

Head, N.

Healer, J.

Hepburn, D.

Heidenescher, J.

Heithcock, G.

Hitz, R.

Hosia, S.

Houlker, Recruit

Hunter, J.

Jackson, M.

Jackson, M.

Janes, S.

Jenkins, E.

Johnson, D.

Johnson, F.

Johnson, S.

Jones, D.

Jones, R.

Jordan, M.

Kennedy, Recruit

Kenybrew, B.

Key, D.
Kolreg, T.
Kraft, J.
Kratzer, W.
Kriebel, D.

Lacik, M.
Lane, F.
Larson, S.
Llamas, L.
Loomis, C.

Lyle, S.
Mann, E.
Mauliola, J.
May, J.
McClain, J.

McKnight, L.
Meronek, M.
Minor, D.
Moberry, T.
Morey, D.

Muron, T.
Murray, I.
Myers, F.
Nelson, T.
Norton, J.

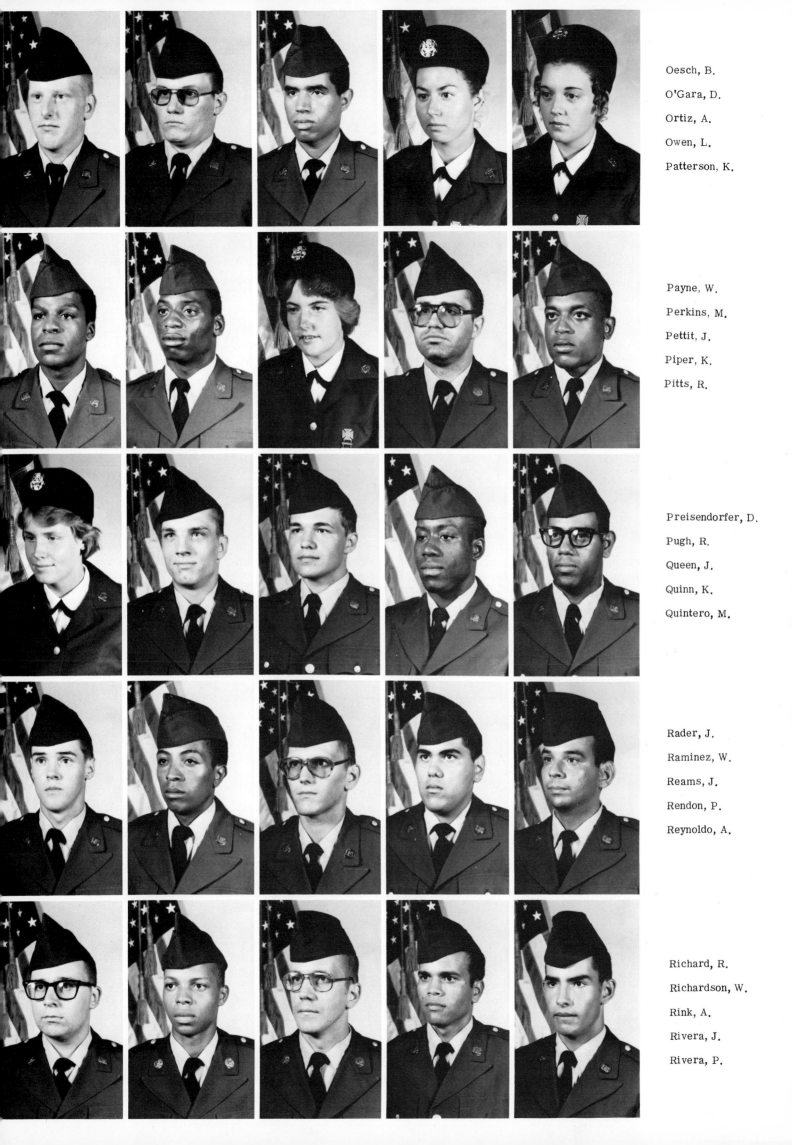

Oesch, B.

O'Gara, D.

Ortiz, A.

Owen, L.

Patterson, K.

Payne, W.

Perkins, M.

Pettit, J.

Piper, K.

Pitts, R.

Preisendorfer, D.

Pugh, R.

Queen, J.

Quinn, K.

Quintero, M.

Rader, J.

Raminez, W.

Reams, J.

Rendon, P.

Reynoldo, A.

Richard, R.

Richardson, W.

Rink, A.

Rivera, J.

Rivera, P.

Robert, T.

Rochan, M.

Rogers, R.

Ross, Recruit

Ross, R.

Rummel, A.

Rurin, K.

Santiago, I.

Scaggs, W.

Scharff, Recruit

Schleicher, S.

Schreiner, P.

Schultz, D.

Schultz, H.

Scoggins, Recruit

Senty, C.

Sharff, D.

Shaw, R.

Shute, E.

Simmons, L.

Skaggs, K.

Skyler, S.

Slocum, C.

Smith, G.

Soreng, M.

Speer, D.

Starr, J.

Stevenson, E.

Stewart, S.

Suella, Recruit

Summers, C.

Sylvara, R.

Thomas, E.

Thornquist, D.

Tincher, T.

Tomlinson, C.

Troup, M.

Tucker, C.

Tucker, D.

Valle, E.

Varela, F.

Walker, L.

Waymer, R.

White, Recruit

Wight, D.

Wilcox, K.

Williams, J.

Williams, S.

Williamson, W.

Wraggs, G.

NIKE-AJAX
MISSILE

LACROSSE
MISSILE